ALASKA

This book was published with generous financial support from the Basque Government.

The Center for Basque Studies and Castillo Suarez would like to thank the Salinas Martínez de Ordoñana family for the use of the image shown on the cover.

Center for Basque Studies
University of Nevada, Reno
1664 North Virginia St,
Reno, Nevada 89557 usa
http://basque.unr.edu

Copyright © 2024 by the Center for Basque Studies and the University of Nevada, Reno
ISBN-13: 978-1-949805-95-6
All rights reserved.

Library of Congress Cataloging-in-Publication Data

Names: Suárez, Castillo, 1976- author. | Olmo, Itxaso del, translator.
Title: Alaska / Castillo Suarez ; translated by Itxaso del Olmo.
Other titles: Alaska. English
Description: Reno : Center for Basque Studies, University of Nevada, 2024. | Series: Basque originals series ; #34 | Summary: "Suarez explores poetry that has also been translated into French, Spanish, Catalan, and Galician and transcends cultural barriers. The title of this book takes inspiration from a roadside hotel named Alaska. It is a place where the author would go when she was a child, a building that has been abandoned for more than two decades now. Much has been written about heartbreak and abandonment, but little about the invisible threads that connect us to places. We all have an Alaska within us, a place chained to our memories reminding us of someone we once loved but we do not know where they are now"-- Provided by publisher.
Identifiers: LCCN 2024038853 (print) | LCCN 2024038854 (ebook) | ISBN 9781949805956 (paperback) | ISBN 9781949805963 (epub)
Subjects: LCSH: Suárez, Castillo, 1976---Translations into English. | LCGFT: Poetry.
Classification: LCC PH5339.S83 A7713 2024 (print) | LCC PH5339.S83 (ebook) | DDC 899/.921--dc23/eng/20240829
LC record available at https://lccn.loc.gov/2024038853
LC ebook record available at https://lccn.loc.gov/2024038854

Printed in the United States of America

ALASKA

CASTILLO SUAREZ

Translated by Itxaso del Olmo

**CENTER FOR BASQUE STUDIES
UNIVERSITY OF NEVADA, RENO**

2024

Basque Original Series #34

Introduction

Sooner or later, winter always comes. Not the snow, though; and you love snowfalls, since they lay bare no more than what is important. But that year it just rained, day after day. The rivers were overflowing, and you stayed in those days, boxing up the life you had had until then.

You decided to distance yourself from friends. Following a rule that is nowhere written, you decided that the friends you had in common would remain his friends after the breakup, as if the person to have known them first would be entitled to do so. That is why they still feel indebted to you in some way: the guilt felt by the one who abandons.

Together with the arrival of the rain, you moved into the guest room, into a small bed. In fact, when you change bedrooms, dreams also change. It seems like you are talking in the language of trees when you are falling asleep, quiet and single-sensed. When you wake up, however, your language is that of birds: you suddenly change direction and fly away.

You have heard that some birds can foresee the rain.

You are boxing up the books. You hold them from the spine and shake them. Purchase receipts fall out every now and then, as well as a dry flower or two. You used to retrieve wildflowers from the lines of recently cut grass, holding on to your uncontrollable tendency to store beauty. It is said that flowers are the last ones to come out in impoverished lands. You click on *Cofrentes* and *Trillo*, the two nuclear plants where your uncle once worked, those two and the word *flowers* next to them. Florist's shops are the first ones to pop up. Then the funeral homes come.

Humidity has softened the paper sheets on the desk. You know you will not be able to rewrite your life, but you are certain you will endure, since we carry on thanks to what hurts us. That is one of the lessons your mother has taught you, even if she has not realized. Suffering the same pain is what makes people grow apart, and it does not bring them closer, although it might seem otherwise.

This year it will not snow. It will, at best, be the sleet that melts before even touching the ground.

When you were kids, you would go all the way to the Alaska, on foot. The hotel parking lot used to be crowded with people passing through. One of the servers was a young ginger man. Dad would always tell you the same thing: the borderline is over there; in the past, there was a chain separating the provinces, which is why this place is called *Katealde*.[1] Nowadays the abandoned hotel can be seen from the highway shoulder. One night, I saw that the neon lights were on, and I thought they might be showing the place to some potential buyer. You often have this dream where you are talking to the young ginger man. But you do not write down dreams.

Most times, dreams come to you while driving, without any means to write them down, looking at the rearview mirror, waiting for a wild boar to appear. You like highways and freeways, not so much the secondary roads, because, when you drive slowly, there is a risk of overthinking, of unintentionally recalling the memories; and, as you very well know, there is nothing we can do to forget what we do not want to remember.

You do not know for how long you have had this instinct not to get attached to anything. When your neighbor came with a sponge cake, willing to talk, you made a great effort to be attentive. She noticed the boxes and bags in the entrance, but she did not ask you when you were leaving the house. It had been a long time since she had last lived in that house, since that night she got out of the car and left for the mountain.

When you empty a home the songs always remain; the friends who advise you to leave the house, those who tell you which house is best to keep; real estate advertisements; doctor's appointments; disappeared languages. When you love someone, you create a language you only use with that person. That language dies when the relationship is over.

We leave our life, our pieces, in people we will not see again. That is why living is about losing those who love us in order to look for them again, in brief. As a matter of fact, when we are loved we feel most strong, even more than when we are actually strong, if you will. But rain comes unexpectedly, just like the interesting people in life. And nothing can be done to stop the rain. In the same way, nothing can be done to hold back the person who decided to abandon you. And, maybe, we feel attracted by the person who is going to abandon us, or the one who has the intention to do so; but the ones who remain with us, whether they decide it or not, they are our prostheses: they are itchy, they also hurt now and then, but without them we would not be able to live.

Sometimes birds are flying all over us, even if we cannot see them.

You do the ironing in the garage. His working tools and uniform have disappeared. Objects disappear and leave an empty space, and we usually need time to get used to the emptiness left by those things, although it is true that what is gone makes room for something else. Life always provides a way to make up for what is lost. A song, for instance. Only in songs do you find someone who gives you everything you need.

You have dreamt about the ginger kid who used to work in the Alaska hotel; he was reading a book, *Orlando*, taking advantage of the fact that there were not many guests. The days you feel down you go to the Alaska, and, just like the Eastern truck drivers back in time, you feel that you are closer to home. You feel that life has fewer sharp edges. That you have all the answers ready, even if no one asks anything.

It is said that Virginia Woolf wanted to comfort her lover Vita Sackville-West with the book *Orlando*, because she had lost her long-time house: Knole House. You keep the paperback edition among the books that you have boxed up. You have two types of books: the ones you bought hoping they would bring you closer to someone, or the ones you got to avoid being fully aware of what was going on around you. You do not know whether to include Woolf's book in the first group or in the second one.

When you are on your own, you are more attentive and you read more *books*.

There is always someone who talks to you about what they are missing. You listen to them carefully, as if there was a way to fill your emptiness with that of their own. This happens with strangers. We all lose our inhibitions when making confessions at airports. And we have all thought about not taking the flight and staying in an unknown city for a long time. But, in the end, nothing happens in that type of journey. You make the return trip thinking that you need to do something about the pain of your fellow travelers, as well as that of your own. You usually have a best seller in your hands, so that no one asks you anything. Normally, nothing happens in your life, and then, everything is happening simultaneously. Therefore, there is no specific moment to stop loving someone. You are on a scale, waiting, and there is someone at home who does not love you, even if you are not yet aware. We know nothing about what is happening to others.

From that moment on, our life is the life of those who have abandoned us. We spend the summers in their swimming pools. The Sunday evenings in their living rooms. It is too early to leave that place and too late to go away.

You have taken your pieces to your parents' house. You do not know how to get rid of what is no longer necessary, what is broken, cracked. You do not know what to do with the ones given to you as a present, and that is why you have invented a new rule: you have taken everything given by someone at some point, without exception. You have no intention of giving anything back, fearing that the fragile connection between words and things could break. You have also kept the messages, which are now meaningless. Unthinkable. Alienated. If you need me, call me. Detaching from the objects would be admitting that no one will come back looking for them. A feeling like seeing the photographs of children whom you had not known until recently. Not having succeeded in making someone happy. The sound of raindrops on the window.

Without realizing it, you are looking for someone who has kept you in mind. In fact, we are connected to those around us by a sewing thread. The thread disappears; not the trace, though. And maybe discerning is accepting you cannot go back. And regretting it because, when you chose someone, you never thought that one day they would not be with you. That the young ginger man was not going to come looking for you in the Alaska parking lot when you got off your bike because it started to rain.

You remember it without a specific order. You do not like the end of winter, but you do like the things that happen during that time, such as the people coming back and forth in a hotel parking lot; without noticing that there is a swimming pool nearby, even if there is no diving board.

You knew he would not be there and yet you went to the Alaska swimming pool.

May it rain and may a small umbrella be enough.

Notes

1 Translator's note: Name formed by the combination of words in Basque *kate* [ˈkæt.e], which means "chain", and *alde* [ˈæld.e] referring to a specific area or a certain space.

Roses

I know about roses,
but I know more about winter flowers.
I know about wounds,
but I know more about bleedings with no injury.
Being without you
is being with whom you could have become,
that I also know;
that love is a rough ocean of words,
grass doesn't grow in midwinter,
and I can't write anything on the window fog.
But the others don't see me this way.
They don't know that I don't own my house:
that the men of my past took it away piece by piece.

Redness

Redness arises in your naked body.
I'll give you nothing to hold in your arms,
nothing, but a blue mallard.
You open my arms,
my guts,
but the muddy snow has taken my insides.
You tell me I'm wild
when you want to hurt me,
for I'd tear your skin off if I could,
and get rid of your stigmas.
My fears are blooming in your naked body.
I can't put your honesty into words.
My scars cannot be seen.

Blood of the Lips

As the blood of my lips
dries on his sheets,
he believes I live with him.
He touches my pale breasts,
says I feel different.
He doesn't know I'm going under the knife
to have my snowy pond removed,
and to be sterilized.
I'm a mare unable to find a shelter.
I've never liked being tied.
I've never met anyone from my same litter.
I've never let anyone touch my mane.
Mine is a life full of snow.
Losses bring nothing in return.

Buds

When animals lose their young,
they beat the ground angrily.
I cried to myself,
and unopened flower buds emerged out of my throat.
I'd choose another death for you.
So you would leave, so everything would change.
Grieving is not something to be understood.
The walls in my heart are made of glass.
You may lose your house, but not your heart.
Mine is an alphabet nobody knows.
There's salt on the roads.
The horse that fell into the river
is fighting against the current.
It has big eyes, just like me.

Fire

After the fever,
I'm ready to molt
to love those with me,
since only what hurts us
can change us.
My heart will burst against a window.
A faraway forest will go up in flames.
Losses will be unarguable,
just like they've been so far;
but there's something I won't lose:
the guilt and my love for winter, both equally.

Red

Oblivion
is the child no one looks at,
the illness brought by cold,
swallowing red and denying it.
Through our thighs we give birth to glaciers,
but when they melt we're far away,
in another sky.
In fact, we never return
to the territories we once owned.
Not because they are not ours,
but because our soil is barren
for the seeds to sprout.

Wounds

No one understands the way I remember,
that I'm in my winter uniform all year round,
that the paths to me are fake.
That before they get to know my secrets,
I throw the young ladies out of my bed
blaming them for not knowing the names of flowers.
No one understands the way I remember:
it's like seeing wounds in the dark.

The Broom Shrub

We read contemptuously in another language.
We want for ourselves the disdain
of dogs trampling on the sown land.
Our battles are as eternal as pointless:
there are women we cannot beat,
and we cannot differ from the written.
Time hides between poems.
As astonishing as snow
is the trace left by silence.
We're unable to return home
fearing we'll find a broom shrub at the entrance
and our footprints on the kitchen floor.
In our memories we had lighter hair.
In our memories it was always summer.
In our memories we would never hit rock bottom.
We've had our hearts patched up since then.
Life tastes like the river bed.

The Fire

As difficult as measuring eucalyptus trees in flames is
understanding the one we love,
or healing a wound with no blood.

The Mortar

Mine is a mortar between cowardice and tenderness,
the quiet, untouched snow.
But if you caressed me with fern,
I'd stick to your house until winter was gone,
just like cattle when they don't want to move around.
I suffered also when I was a child:
I wanted to swallow the planets, eyes closed,
so no new season would come by.
I still couldn't see the beauty of destruction,
couldn't see that nothing depends on fate.

Photographs

I'm afraid of the gut feeling before giving birth,
since they won't be able to tear out what they've left inside me.
I'm searching for the photograph where I look beautiful.
I embellish the past,
embellish it, so there's no need to see it again.
I don't know how I'm going to think back without photographs,
since memories in photographs no longer belong to us.
I'm made of the little pieces of books I've read,
of places I'd want to visit,
of places I'd take you to.

The Definition of Love

Love is the place where one's memories
meet the other's.
However, those whom we feel
are narrating our life
decide to go quiet
sometimes.

Exuding Fear

I've never gotten far from the ground.
I don't remember what frightens me,
but I live exuding fear.
I'd like to run away,
but I have nothing to escape from.
You're lying by my side:
two solitudes are never a single one.
Just like wounded animals, my frights protect me.
And I don't know whether I'm the very one you've known.
The lost beloved never disappear;
they are absent or they'll be someone else.
Living is leaving footprints in the snow:
spoiling what's beautiful,
bringing to light what we want covered,
accepting downfalls.

Finding an Animal Shot

When driving in the rain, I think that the journey will last forever,
that I won't find the way back home,
and I'll show up at an empty restaurant by the side of the road,
and I'll want to be myself and not anyone else.
If I could leave the sniper position
and choose what to be afraid of,
I'd ask those who don't need me
to love me
or to just keep walking away.
In fact,
falling in love is like finding an animal shot:
you'd escape from there if you could,
but you stay looking at the way the blood keeps melting the snow.

My Guilt

I know summer has arrived when I'm missing my will to talk.
When I don't have to shovel the snow to move my car.
I notice only the things that hurt.
I had a heart with no beating within me,
which passed away the same way a fly dies in an air conditioning unit.
I know it stopped beating in the city,
on a Monday;
I don't know whether it was me,
or my barren thoughts.
Tied to something I hadn't known until I mourned him,
I choose the books I want to read.
But wounds heal quickly if they are fresh.
My guilt is like the one of the people who look happy:
nice photographs don't necessarily mean nice things.
Chance is artificial in its most me-like meaning.
Only in a place found within my womb
is the language of beasts silent.

Dedications

The sunburn on the shoulders
disappears,
but I'm still struggling
with the words written in drizzle.
The fear of failing again
prevents me from recalling
the things that made me sad before.
Rain covers nothing.
The man who nearly loved me
would fuck me when I was pregnant.
The man I love the most
makes love to me despite knowing I'm barren.
They both push me and make me nauseous.
We've had sex in silence to make it look more beautiful.
I don't like the beach too much,
or the mountain.
I don't want dedications
because they resemble my tears.

Shelter

I live here
but my heaven is over there.
I don't fully own what I love,
and because of that I love even more.
Through the swimming pool lanes
I quietly carry a knot of gametes
as the mute always demands silence.
I don't notice simple things until they hurt me,
until they fade away.
The body is what I am.
The womb is what I am not going to be.
You won't be able to sneak in and you won't be able to protect me.
I came to feed other ways of life
without being part of them.
You sleep with me.
You'd like to make a stay at my body,
even if I won't let you in.
You know I won't do as you command me.
I'll never be shelter for your offspring.

Autobiography

One of the first things I was taught
was how to swim,
so that I wouldn't feel overwhelmed
when approaching the beach.
But instead of disappearing in the water,
I used to stay in the changing rooms and write
what would later on become poems.
We despise the things that look like us,
and our grandmother didn't want another writer at home;
since writing is killing a wild animal with the car:
there's no going back,
you can't get it off your mind.
It's like the first time you're told
that you're not loved;
you don't know what to write,
whether a poem or a testament;
you don't know who loves you less: them or yourself.
Your mind is in constant fervor from that moment on,
similar to the restlessness the day before a trip,
which leads you to write subordinate sentences.
The one who's infertile keeps alive in my notebooks.

Poetics

A scar has no other purpose but to recall the wound.
They are neither beautiful nor useful.
Very similar to poems, then.
It could be said they are the same thing.

Snow Mood

I can't find an explanation for this snow mood in me.
Maybe it's because I feel hurt by
summer memories,
reefs,
channels,
Augusts,
children unable to invent a thing,
life partners abandoning you with accurate words,
lovers who don't respond to kisses,
hospitals,
heparin shots.
I don't know why I love the snow
if it's not letting me get used to the cold.

The Inside-out Wound

Revealing our own self,
we have no other option sometimes.
To expose our veins,
and to deny the descendants the option to live.
To dismantle furniture, to empty the house.
Not to think where and with whom to spend this summer.
If you come looking for me,
you won't find me on the way home.
Catfish can be felt in my empty womb.
They scare you,
but you love the distance separating me from the rest.
Interrupted beginnings bind us to the earth.

To Be Someone Else

I had my lungs filled up with bramble by the time I met you.
I was a beach hidden in high tide.
I couldn't undress before you,
for fear of your finding my inner depths.
I've always wished I were someone else,
renewing my skin every year and dropping the worn pieces.
I've always wished I were a tamed animal,
following straight lines,
finding comfort in safe spaces.
More docile than I've been.
I've always wished
I could return the pieces in big waste bags
to those longing to live clinging on to me,
up to the point of becoming strangers.
Crying for once will turn me into someone else, you say;
that it leaves no trace,
unless it's on the scaled skin of fish.
That the loneliness of being great is not just mine.

Rituals

At times, it feels like some things are not important and do not mean anything. And you suddenly find an abandoned nest on your way. And there is no going back. All the places you cannot go back to come to your mind. There is no way to decline the set of words we have to name the uprooting. Perhaps because you belong to a house taken by the waters of a reservoir, your rituals never change: every summer, you read the quotations written down in your notebook, the ones from the poetry books you had read long ago and did not remember. You hibernate, just like the alfalfa plant. Thinking about the name of a baby who might not be born marks the beginning of something you do not know yet. You are not sure whether life was easier before, but you used to find shelter to breathe in all those pains you carry within. You were not yet aware that the pain wanted to spread all over your body.

Scars

I could become you,
the young woman you met that summer night,
and count your footprints some other night
until we touched each other.
For there are no two identical nights,
but in any of them can the skin be regenerated with another piece of skin.
Call it a scar if you like.
The skin forgets nothing,
like that young woman crying in the park,
sad and lonely, both at the same time.
My ashes always take me to your fires.
To the showers shared with you.
My scars don't hurt.
The further I get,
the lonelier I should feel,
but I'm the type of person like those who put on make-up every day,
like the ones who don't believe in a death that is not perceivable.
Like those who don't let on about the houses they've lived in.

Open Wound

Bumping into my own self could be the only option.
Making a bouquet with all the questions I won't ask.
Disappearing behind a poem written in the language of plants.
To stop loving the snow.
Leaving a good mooring as a legacy for those who don't understand me.
To lock my contradictions in a cloakroom.
To create an invisible child
without causing wrinkles in my breasts,
without tying my entrails to the umbilical cord.
I could be a semantic mistake,
but mine is an open wound,
one with no chance to heal.

Lonely Children

All lonely children are alike in one way:
they never utter words of love,
as if they were barren,
just like love itself.
They have an incomprehensible bond with queues
whether at airports or supermarkets,
since they love waiting.
It feels like they are not here.
They emanate an earthy aroma,
are the keepers of all unspoken things,
and write affectionless poems
in adulthood.
Damage is not the same for everyone,
but love poems do return.
They always come back
to rebuild the dictionary.

Appointments

I don't want to attend doctors' appointments,
because I don't want to tell them I have green eyes
due to the beech trees I conceal in full humidity.
Tell them I fill up with fog the beds I don't own
and take away the sleep of those staying in my shadow.
Tell them I'm growing with low light,
in the exile of the things lost.
Tell them I'm constantly fighting with my poems,
because they pretend to be me,
because they attend the appointments instead of me,
even the doctors' ones.

The Stages of Grief

Not wanting to write about you
To stop seeking your love
Counting the empty spaces in the closets
Not making plans on special occasions
Buying raffia bags to carry the pieces
Cleaning the refrigerator shelves
Spending my evenings at the library
Wearing socks to sleep
Sleeping on the single bed in the guest room
Wishing to feel alone and not being able to
Looking for someone else's love
Writing about you

Desires

Opening my eyes and seeing no marks on my body
in a place where you and I are not,
without feeling cold.
This is what desires are like:
they force you to start again,
to let your hair grow,
to push away the people who can't love you,
to make room for the pain in the everyday tasks,
to face you and get my lungs trapped with tor-grass.
Desires are like that:
as necessary as useless.
Because you keep buying big bottles of soap,
you keep starting relationships backwards,
hiding like a deadly wounded animal.
Waiting to die.
Waiting to be found.

(Falling Out of) Love

This is what (falling out of) love is like.
You invite them to your place,
and end up sleeping in the guest room yourself.

Wild Animal

The most difficult things to understand are the last ones to forget.
That is why the lost things remain with us for a long time.
They are not actually with us,
but we look at them
the way we look at the swimmers in empty swimming pools.
That's why the abandoned ones never lose their identity.
That's why grieving has no ending.
We want to pull out the memories that come to our mind
when we strip off the ornamental ivy from the wall at home
and it looks ruined.
It's impossible to escape from the things lost.
That leads us to leave the bedroom door open,
so the night is over as soon as possible;
leads us to love the snow-covered landscapes,
since we're also dressed up in our grieves,
just like the snow.
We don't measure time in hours;
we count the deaths of people close to us
when we update our planners.
You and I are now strangers.
You and I sleep in other people's beds.
We build blood reefs so as not to have children
and to have no one to cry for.
All the women we have been
are a wild animal hiding in the brambles,
one that shows up in a house by the roadside,
in another town.

The Language of Beasts

I spoke the language of beasts.
Like a mare hiding under the fog,
I used to be missing for days.
I'd only let the branches touch my skin.
I'd shiver under the rain.
Few were the memories I kept,
barely enough so I could return to you.
You'd take me as a docile animal on my return,
with pity and sorrow.
Barefoot in the snow.
Not knowing what to do with what you didn't have.

A Dead Dove

Years can go by in one night
and a dead dove can appear on the pillow
bidding the last farewell.
The emptied bed is then emptied again.
You realize that you'll always be a runaway,
that your nets have never been like someone else's,
and those waiting for you are never in your dovecote.
Then you write,
so that the written words help you live,
since writing has always been easier than collecting nets.

In the Sparse Forest

The shade of the beech trees is the size of your eyes,
dark and thick,
one which doesn't get undressed until autumn.
The way back home has been covered by leaves
and you're a dog lost in the rain, looking for shelter.
A piece of me remains in the sparse forest,
in the rain,
held by a gut feeling,
because I want to give birth my way
in the midst of a lunging storm,
without having my womb dilated.

Right Whale

I want to learn something
no one will teach me,
such as
how to pull out the harpoons stuck in my heart
without causing any bleeding.
Mine is the skin of a whale.
I carry a colony of barnacles
that will remain on the surface after my death,
swimming,
showing.

Draining

You told me to go
because you knew you wouldn't come after me
when I looked at the screens in the airport.
You let me know you would leave,
after draining all I had told you
up to becoming someone else.
I'd like to write something to get back to you,
to draw a line of words on your chest
and graft my poems on your skin.
I don't know who you will be,
but I'm waiting for you anyway.

The Beauty of Cold

Cracks always become wider,
and memories blurrier.
We can foresee the storm coming sooner and sooner,
but noticing neglect keeps getting harder and harder.
Even so, when we're left aside,
our resentment comes into words
and it stays with us.
Ice burns the leaves,
but not the flowers.
We used to be brittle,
and now we're resilient instead.
As long as the beauty of cold lasts,
so will we.
Until we realize that the one we're missing
will not come again.

The Underwater Flower

You're an underwater flower,
I'd rather not know that you're in the sea,
that you are food for some fish
and shelter for others.
I'd rather not know what's going on
between you and me.
I'd rather pretend I don't see your mysteries.
I don't know who you truly are,
but I'd rather leave it as it is.

Where to Go Looking for Me

I came to deprive you of breath with my gills,
to scratch your skin with my bones,
to replace your rage with my oblivion.
Since it's easier to choose the ones I love or hate
than to stop bearing those who love or hate me.
Because I don't want to get used to having my guts tangled,
used to looking far away so no one knows where to seek me.
I'm aware that giving up is never
a better option than agreeing on not hating.
Aware that it's hard to choose who we'll have to be,
that it's difficult to choose a city to live in, one that is not sad.
Loneliness has chased us wherever we went.
We complete the poems by peeling off the ones missing and the ones gone,
and we do so with one single goal:
to turn around and find no one there.

Artificial Snow

I don't know when, but one day it'll snow artificially.
I'll swallow hanks of yarn until my guts are swollen up,
and I'll menstruate a glacier.
The scared one is always waiting to feel the cold.
I'll open my vagina so you come in again;
so your pain remains instead of mine.

An Air Plant

Even with this vacuum-sealed wound,
I've put away
the winter clothes,
the toiletry bag,
the silence between us,
the fear of going back home and you finding me,
the half-written poems,
the traces of you being at home,
the ultrasound scans,
the spice jars.
Every night I stare at myself
because an air plant has sprouted under my skin
in a few weeks' time.
Without you and at my expense.

A German Car

A surgical wound needs two weeks to heal.
You need two birthdays to forget someone you love.
Two weeks and ten heparin shots.
Two birthdays and a German car.

A Supermarket

Just like in a supermarket,
I have nothing on the first row of the shelf;
but I always keep the simplest topics far away
and the toughest ones handy.
I'm waiting for the next stocktaking,
so I check what I'm lacking.

Yearning for Snow

Sometimes it seems like I've come to set fire to the dark woods.
My mind is about to deflagrate
and I begin to argue over the love words.
Sometimes I'm a foreigner at my birthplace
because the hunting dogs don't recognize me.
They sense that I've come to put a strain on their peace.
Sometimes the snow reaches the beach,
snow over snow,
and I begin to swallow the whiteness
so as to find my name on the sand:
here is the woman who lives yearning for snow,
the observer of silence,
her own foe.

Extra Life

I've always been afraid of mental illnesses,
of car accidents,
of those who want to know me better than I do,
of my parents' death,
of stone-made retaining walls,
of pregnancy tests,
of rereading my poems
–even if literature is my complementary life–,
of swampy soils,
of hotel rooms
–each room being for individual use–.
However, I can lose friends and responsibilities,
I can live with grief,
without measuring the phases and the periods,
because I've got used to living against my heart.

Living

At our age
we know all we're going to learn about friendship:
that we won't become better as friends;
that, if anything, we'll get worse.
We didn't know whether we were saying goodbye or not,
but we knew by then
that we can't do anything to be loved
or to stop someone from loving us.
Reality, unsweetened, can't keep up with a poem.
We'd like to be rescued by those we want,
so that we cling to their legs
just like a child launching at us.
But no.
Someone else's children are of no one's interest.
We'll plunge into a hibernating state
in a pricey apartment with no balcony.
If we're not loved
there's nothing to do.
We don't remember what we've dreamt,
but it's not necessary.
A sniper won't tell us where they're going to stand,
but we can tell they're out there.
We'll write because we don't feel too comfortable.
Because it makes us indestructible.
We're angry,
and we don't want to say why,
as if that made us weaker.
We cannot understand
what makes
the people we once loved
become strangers,
but,
eventually,
living
is learning what's happening to us.
That, and choosing who we want to keep nearby.

A Swimming Pool in Your Bedroom

It seemed like it was all fine,
but there was so much going on:
whatever you did,
you thought that you were failing,
that you were in the wrong place.
You'd worry about the future
and your greatest enemy was nostalgia.
You built a swimming pool in your bedroom.
But, suddenly, with an unexpected storm
you realized that you were not telling the truth when you were writing,
that, when choosing whether to tell or not to tell,
you were dismissing something:
what was about to happen or what was happening,
and you didn't want to know about it.
You'd dream of the beaches of an island,
although you knew it'd be difficult to escape from there
because the *Posidonia* would chain your legs.
You realized you'd be forced to forget all you had read;
since writing was like looking at the bright side of a disaster.
You wanted to touch the water with a finger,
but you didn't manage to do it.
You gathered all the places where you were not
and those where you should be:
that's where you had been at some point.
A place where more people lived than there was room for.

The Chancre

All the chestnut trees died of a disease.
We lost the words to name the chancre.
We didn't feel any sorrow,
since those trees take a long time
to bear fruits or lumber.
When the danger and the fear are gone,
we'll return to the city
to write about the trails closed by depopulation.
We're interested in poetry
because it doesn't tell anything.

Family Tree

Sometimes, a family tree can be too short,
and the risk of feeling too proud of yourself, quite big.
You remain alive but with nothing to hold on to.
Dead fish come to the surface in the meantime.
You overcome the fear of loneliness,
but chained to that loneliness.
You listen to music nonstop, but without understanding the lyrics.
There are very good lyrics and very bad poems.
And vice versa.

Protopoems and Discarded Ones

How much you've changed only you know,
but the outsiders haven't noticed the change.
You've changed so much.
You've tried hard to change.
Now you get chapped lips in just a moment.
You get chapped lips
when a stranger kisses you.
When you stay over at mom's,
you find protopoems and discarded ones in the nightstand.
You count the decisions you've made so that you fall asleep,
and you realize that the best things
were brought by the wrong decisions.
You feel the same as when you first slept with a woman
and left your clothes on the floor.
That feeling can't be kept for long,
that's to say, having no one around.

A White Calla Lily

While holding a white calla lily,
I realize
that I love more and more nameless things,
that silence consumes my surroundings,
that I have my desk empty,
and I endure pain with no extra effort.
I even forget that my inner wetland is right here,
that enemies keep piling up in my journal,
that I lost a big war at home
and the traces of trenches remain there.
While holding a white calla lily
I realize
that no one writes about new loves,
but they do, instead, about the ones lost.
While holding a white calla lily,
I realize
that I too have a single flower,
a toxic one, if eaten raw.

A Heart of Earth

Just like a stateless person crossing the border,
or a nomad,
I walk side to side along the beach,
under the sun,
in the opposite direction,
waiting for a soldier with no name
or a captain with no navy
to show up.
We won't talk about misfortune;
nor about joy.
We won't confess to each other
that we're waiting for a whale to come ashore,
one dragged and wounded by a ship,
one that made it to the land,
to those of us who have a heart of earth.

Waiting for the Light

You slept in my bed,
but your mind went out to the street sweepers when the day broke
or following those who go to work in any other direction,
in order to not bear all the feelings of loneliness.
The one we love the most we love in silence
since words may lead to disappointment sooner or later.
Just like a flower,
you dried out and left your seed on my sheets,
waiting for the light.

Epilogue (although it could also be the prologue)

It is never too late to start from scratch
as long as I have books, snow, and friends;
those, and a good car to go anywhere.
To a tundra with Igor Estankona,
to make a list of the titles a book could have,
and also of the people we want to keep with us.
To the Red City with Asier Serrano,
even if we swore to each other
we wouldn't endure the same pain twice
and we wouldn't return to that cruel city.
To the cemetery of Lekeitio with Miren Agur Meabe,
to complete the book on the botany of love
and to chisel an epitaph for us.
To the port of Ondarroa with Leire Bilbao,
to rinse off each other's oil, blood, and scales,
and to rewrite our skin.
It will never be too late for me to write about life, death, and love,
to arrange photographs,
to tell you all that I love you.

Milton Keynes UK
Ingram Content Group UK Ltd.
UKHW021926281024
450365UK00017B/987